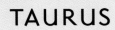

TAURUS

TAURUS

21 April–21 May

PATTY GREENALL & CAT JAVOR

MQP

Published by MQ Publications Limited
12 The Ivories
6–8 Northampton Street
London N1 2HY
Tel: 020 7359 2244
Fax: 020 7359 1616
Email: mail@mqpublications.com
www.mqpublications.com

Copyright © MQ Publications Limited 2004
Text copyright © Patty Greenall & Cat Javor 2004

Illustrations: Gerry Baptist

ISBN: 1-84072-654-7

1 3 5 7 9 0 8 6 4 2

Printed in Italy

WHAT IS ASTROLOGY?

Astrology is the practice of interpreting the positions and movements of celestial bodies with regard to what they can tell us about life on Earth. In particular it is the study of the cycles of the Sun, Moon, and the planets of our solar system, and their journeys through the twelve signs of the zodiac—Aries, Taurus, Gemini, Cancer, Leo, Virgo, Libra, Scorpio, Sagittarius, Capricorn, Aquarius, and Pisces—all of which provide astrologers with a rich diversity of symbolic information and meaning.

Astrology has been labeled a science, an occult magical practice, a religion, and an art, yet it cannot be confined by any one of these descriptions. Perhaps the best way to describe it is as an evolving tradition.

Throughout the world, for as far back as history can inform us, people have been looking up at the skies and attaching stories and meanings to what they see there. Neolithic peoples in Europe built huge stone structures such as Stonehenge in southern England in order to plot the cycles of the Sun and Moon, cycles that were so important to a fledgling agricultural society. There are star-lore traditions in the ancient cultures of India, China, South America, and Africa, and among the indigenous people of Australia. The ancient Egyptians plotted the rising of the star Sirius, which marked the annual flooding of the Nile, and in ancient Babylon, astronomer-priests would perform astral divination in the service of their king and country.

Since its early beginnings, astrology has grown, changed, and diversified into a huge body of knowledge that has been added to by many learned men and women throughout history. It has continued to evolve and become richer and more informative, despite periods when it went out of favor because of religious, scientific, and political beliefs.

Offering us a deeper knowledge of ourselves, a profound insight into what motivates, inspires, and, in some cases, hinders, our ability to be truly our authentic selves, astrology equips us better to make the choices and decisions that confront us daily. It is a wonderful tool, which can be applied to daily life and our understanding of the world around us.

The horoscope—or birth chart—is the primary tool of the astrologer and the position of the Sun, Moon, Mercury, Venus, Mars, Jupiter, Saturn,

Uranus, Neptune, and Pluto at the moment a person was born are all considered when one is drawn up. Each planet has its own domain, affinities, and energetic signature, and the aspects or relationships they form to each other when plotted on the horoscope reveal a fascinating array of information. The birth, or Sun, sign is the sign of the zodiac that the Sun was passing through at the time of birth. The energetic signature of the Sun is concerned with a person's sense of uniqueness and self-esteem. To be a vital and creative individual is a fundamental need, and a person's Sun sign represents how that need most happily manifests in that person. This is one of the most important factors taken into account by astrologers. Each of the twelve Sun signs has a myriad of ways in which it can express its core meaning. The more a person learns about their individual Sun sign, the more they can express their own unique identity.

ZODÏAC WHEEL

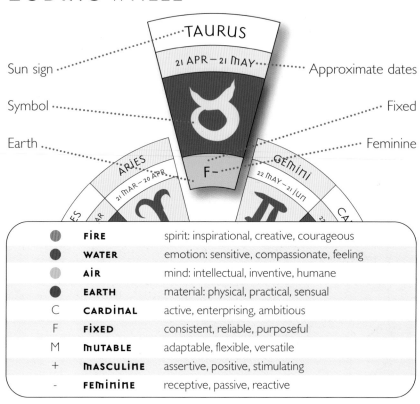

Sun sign .... TAURUS

21 APR – 21 MAY .... Approximate dates

Symbol .... Fixed

Earth .... Feminine

ARÏES
21 MAR – 20 APR

GEMÏNÏ
22 MAY – 21 JUN

F–

◑	**FÏRE**	spirit: inspirational, creative, courageous
●	**WATER**	emotion: sensitive, compassionate, feeling
◔	**AÏR**	mind: intellectual, inventive, humane
●	**EARTH**	material: physical, practical, sensual
C	**CARDÏNAL**	active, enterprising, ambitious
F	**FÏXED**	consistent, reliable, purposeful
M	**MUTABLE**	adaptable, flexible, versatile
+	**MASCULÏNE**	assertive, positive, stimulating
-	**FEMÏNÏNE**	receptive, passive, reactive

PART ONE

THE ESSENTIAL TAURUS

RULERSHIPS

Taurus is the second sign of the zodiac, the first of the Earth signs, and is ruled by the planet Venus. Taurus is also one of the four Fixed signs and its symbol is the Bull, an animal known for its hard work and natural instincts. The horns of the bull have been compared with the crescent moon, which has an affinity to Taurus because both represent the feminine. There are earthly correspondences of everything in life for each of the Sun signs. The part of the human body that Taurus represents is the neck. Gemstones for Taurus are emerald, blue topaz, malachite, and lapis lazuli. Taurus relates to the color green and the metal copper, and also signifies farms, pastures, cattle, stables, banks, bankers, money, jewelry, art and art dealers, daisies, forget-me-nots, lilies, moss, and spinach.

TAURUS

The part of the human body that
Taurus represents is the neck.

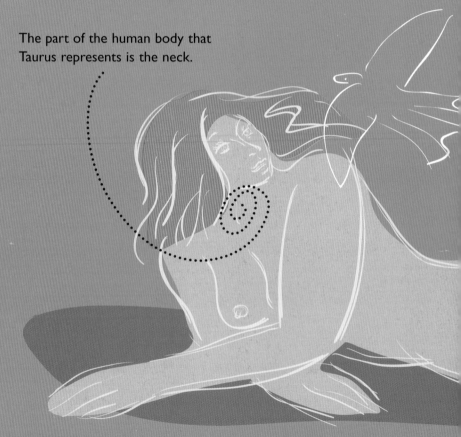

Banks, bankers, cash, jewelry

Farms, pastures, cattle, stables

art dealers

PERSO⊙NALiTY

Those born under the sign of Taurus are the strong, silent type. They're so composed and apparently so tranquil that they emanate a sense of solid security. Even the occasional chatty Taureans always sound measured and deliberate when they speak. They are not uncomfortable with silence and don't open their mouths just to make a noise, but instead they really think about what they want to say before they say it.

Taureans have a reputation for being slow, plodding, and even lazy, but this is not at all the case. Yes, they deal with new experiences at a leisurely pace, but that's because it's very important to them to understand exactly what's going on. They are truly physical and rely on their physical senses to inform themselves about the world around them, listening, looking, and touching in order to measure and assess before making a judgment. Taureans are never hasty when making a decision; they are careful and cautious because making a mistake means going back to the beginning and starting all over again. So if something can't be touched, smelled, tasted, or seen, then it's unlikely Taurus will spend much time thinking about it. It's not that they don't respect, or aren't curious about, more conceptual matters, only that life is so rich in terms of physical experience that they prefer not to waste their time on what might be seen as whimsical or nonsensical. But this does not rule out their passion for romance, art, and music. Since they are ruled by the planet Venus, they are susceptible to beauty in all its forms, and are known for their abundant creativity and appreciation of creativity in others.

Indeed, many Taurus people can be found working in the world of the arts, sometimes as performers or artists themselves, but just as often on the business or promotional side. Their creativity can be just as evident in the fields of agriculture, banking, and restaurants, and they make excellent wine-merchants and interior decorators.

Taureans are tenacious and determined and will push on with a project until it's either completed or all of its potential has been exhausted. Their stamina and stoic nature give them greater staying power in the kind of difficult situation that has other, less determined, people quitting or walking away. That is the secret of Taurus success: they're able to get on with things, stick at a problem and, through sheer stubbornness, usually achieve their ambitions. In fact, being stubborn is one of the main accusations aimed at those born under the Fixed sign of Taurus. It's true that it would take a herd of wild elephants to shift them from any position they hold dear, but since they feel that they've spent time and effort reaching that position, no one should blame them for not wanting to give it up.

A sense of possession and ownership are also very important to the Taurus personality: material objects represent both achievement and feelings of security. Their home is often a place of retreat and they adore the sensation of being surrounded by things they've earned and paid for themselves, although gifts from others represent acceptance and love and so are also cause for pride and happiness. There's always a sense of comfort and luxury—indulgences that Taurus just can't do without—in the Taurus environment, and the refrigerator is usually well stocked, particularly with what is often described as "comfort food." They appreciate quality even more than quantity, so even if their home isn't packed with possessions, you can be sure that what they do have is well-made, durable, and probably rather expensive. They have a really powerful need to indulge, luxuriate in, and partake of the finer things in life, hence they love the trappings of wealth, whether in the form of expensive French perfume, costly soft furnishings, or fine wine and dining.

The tendency to overindulge means that Taureans need to keep an eye on their weight. They'll go a long way to cater to the hedonistic side of their character because physical pleasure in all its forms makes them feel confident, safe, and secure. When a bull is feeling insecure, it's uncomfortable, and when it's uncomfortable, it becomes unpredictable, which is when it's at its most vulnerable. Taurus people don't like feeling vulnerable, since that's when other people think they can push them around, and if pushed too far, they become angry. A bull on the rampage is a frightening sight! All that power and strength can cause an awful lot of damage. It's a demolition army of one. Taureans can be as tenacious, thorough, and determined in demolishing something as they can be at creating it. Thankfully, going on the rampage is a very rare occurrence since it takes an enormous amount of provocation before the laid-back, peaceful Taurus will go so far as to lose control.

But pleasure for Taurus isn't just physical. It doesn't stop at sitting on a comfortable sofa with a glass of wine and a tub of ice-cream. They crave affection as much as they crave chocolate and enjoy the physical presence and touch of a loved one. Romance is the name of the game. Candlelight, flowers, and soft music do much to soothe the beast in them, and when they set their sights on a potential lover, they show their usual determination to woo the object of their affections and win their heart. It's hard to imagine a more committed, loyal, and trustworthy lover than a Taurus in a mutually devoted relationship. Of course, the relationship may not always work out the way they want and when that happens, their possessiveness and jealousy are not very appealing. But if things don't work out, you can be sure it won't be for Taurus's lack of effort or commitment. As friends, Taureans demonstrate the same degree of support and affection. They are dependably calm, patient, and caring.

CAREER & MONEY

Taurus is aware of the practicalities of life, which includes a consciousness of the value of money. It would be unusual to see a Taurus spend frivolously—they simply don't do it, unless they have specifically allocated money to it. They know the meaning of working for life's rewards and are ideal employees—dependable, trustworthy, and persistent. Once Taureans get into a job, they stick to it, especially if they are being paid! They are good with money because they tend not to get emotionally involved with it, though they enjoy the things that money can buy and know how to save and invest. In all probability, the world of banking, stocks, shares, and finance is full of people with a Taurus influence in their birth charts because they all have a knack for handling money well. Career-wise, Taureans make excellent property developers and builders and they can be successful farmers and gardeners. Ruled by Venus, they also have an affinity for the arts and make wonderful musicians, sculptors, jewelers, upholsterers, tailors, and designers.

It's a pleasure to do business with Taureans because they keep their word and can be relied on. However, if changes need to be made to what has already been agreed, they may dig their heels in and, if they really feel pushed, they may become physical! It takes a lot to arouse the temper of this warm-hearted Bull but if it does happen, it would be best to run away and wait until they cool down, firstly, because they can't run very fast, and secondly, because they are very forgiving even though they never forget. You can rely on the otherwise good-natured Taurus to give you another chance; after all, they prefer to work with what they have rather than begin completely afresh. All of this means that they are staunchly loyal but they also demand total faithfulness from co-workers. They say what they mean and mean what they say, putting all their cards on the table and keeping everything above board. Everyone else had better do the same too!

To say that Taureans can't go very fast is not exactly true; they just need to do things at their own speed. With so many attributes, Taureans are very much valued both as employees and bosses, but they do sometimes need to be able to adapt to other methods of working. This is about the only sticking point for them but if they can overcome it, they will undoubtedly win the "Employee of the Year" award time and again, whether they are at the top of the work pyramid or somewhere closer to the bottom.

THE TAURUS **CHİLD**

From almost the moment they come into the world, it's easy to see how much Taurus children depend on comfort and security. This is a child who thrives on displays of physical affection. Soft words and cooing noises are inadequate without an accompanying gentle touch or firm hug. The Taurus child needs to feel safe and secure before attempting independent actions, such as walking and talking. For this reason, they may appear to be slow in exhibiting these skills, but in truth they just need to be sure that they'll get it right first time. Often they will surprise loved ones by suddenly saying a word clearly or performing a task with a steady hand that they had not been able to do the day before. This tendency carries on throughout childhood. It's almost impossible to hurry them along against their own better judgment. If parents or friends attempt to do so, all that happens is that their willful stubbornness gets provoked and they become less, not more, likely to complete a task quickly. This remains true whether it's cleaning their room or trying out a new maneuver on the jungle gym.

With their gentle, cheerful charm, their sense of commitment, and their commonsense approach, Taureans tend to be rather popular at school although they usually prefer to hang out with a select, reliable group of close friends. As they grow into adolescence, their powerful determination to assert their will becomes more prominent. When ordered to do something by a parent or teacher, the word "no" is frequently heard in response. It's not that they're deliberately disagreeable, only that unless the reason for doing something is explained to them clearly, they see no point in doing it in order to please somebody else. As long as young Taureans are not simply being stubborn for stubbornness' sake, their calm, loving nature makes them a comfort and a joy to have around.

PERFECT GiFTS

When choosing gifts for Taureans, the one thing to keep in mind is that they are ruled by lovely Venus, so they like things that are pleasing to the senses and esthetically gratifying, but preferably also practical and durable. If, for example, they would like some wine glasses, they would prefer crystal to ordinary glass. If it's jewelry, anything expensive will suit.

Taureans appreciate beauty and quality, so whether it's golf clubs or cream cakes, only the finest will do. If this is beyond your budget, don't despair. A few delicious handmade chocolates will be greatly appreciated and will cost no more than an entire box of ordinary candy. They like gifts that make them feel cherished—something with a romantic theme such as an ornament engraved with words of undying love. But remember, too, that the gift should also be practical, so silver flatware or beautiful but usable one-of-a-kind cups and saucers will be preferred to something purely decorative, unless that something ties in perfectly with their interior decor.

Clothing? Taurus rules the neck, so a cashmere scarf or a luxury pashmina shawl would be well received. Naturally, a necklace is just the ticket, and one of green gemstones, particularly emeralds, would be most appreciated.

FAVORITE FOODS

The deliciously indulgent Taurus is easily the gourmet chef's best friend. For Taurus, sitting down to a meal is a pleasure that is not to be hurried; every morsel must be savored, every mouthful is sacred. Indeed, food often becomes a hobby for many people born under the sign of the Bull. They strike up friendships with the chefs and staff at their favorite restaurants so that they are always in the know about what is most delicious on the menu of the day. Their taste for rich foods and fine wines is not so much a luxury as a necessity. From a very early age, Taureans derive a sense of security from having their appetites satisfied, and although they aren't fussy about trying new flavors and different types of dishes, they will feel cheated if the food has not been prepared with all due care and attention.

A full cooked breakfast is just what Taureans need to set them up for the day and give them a warm glow, but if time doesn't permit, then they're just as happy doing without. Eating on the run is sacrilege, although sitting down to snack between meals is something most Taurus people indulge in at sometime or another. There is no set pattern to their eating preferences except that their lunch and evening meal should be of the highest quality and should be served in style and in comfortable surroundings. They also have a notoriously sweet tooth and must take care not to embarrass the sweet trolley with their lascivious glances throughout a meal.

FASHION & **STYLE**

Taureans might not have an extensive wardrobe, but what they do have will be of the best quality. They would never be seen wearing cheap garments that fall apart in the first wash and will rarely, if ever, have clothes made from synthetic fibers: only natural fibers, such as cotton, linen, and silk will do! They like their clothes to be robust and comfortable since they're not the type to slavishly follow the latest trend or fashion. They do, however, enjoy poring over glossy magazines, where they can see what the top fashion houses are offering each season. They have expensive tastes, and yet they manage to convey an effortless elegance. Taurus women do seem to prefer trousers, for the simple reason that they're practical, while the men want clothes that they don't have to bother pressing and ironing.

Rich, earthy colors suit them best—all shades of green, plus brown, beige, and off-white. Taureans can also look fabulous in the more muted colors of spring, such as dusky pink and blue. And this is one sign that can really get away with patterned fabrics, whether bold or subtle, although they probably prefer to offset the pattern with blocks of solid color.

It's always possible to spot Taurus people from their stylishly disheveled appearance, but look closely and it will soon be obvious that one single item of their clothing, although old and well worn, has probably cost more than most people's entire outfits!

iDEAL **HOMES**

Sumptuous comfort is Taurus's homestyle theme. The home must not only be practical but also easy to live in, and must look good and be a source of pride. Taurus individuals have rigid standards for their home and how they keep it. They tend to put things back where they belong so they don't end up with a week's worth of dirty linen strewn everywhere, but although they are clean and tidy, they are not fastidious.

Their home is a place where everything works and looks good as well. They don't ignore things like chipped plates, frayed towels, or the curtain rail that was never put up properly, and will replace something if it needs replacing or fix it themselves if it needs fixing. Theirs is a home that's big on comfort but their idea of "comfort" means "fit for a king to drop in at a moment's notice." Yet despite this, everyone is made welcome and no one would feel out of place, not even the local hobo.

And finally, don't forget that Taurus loves luxury—though not to excess. They have a strong esthetic sense yet they're incredibly practical. In order to get an idea of what a Taurus home looks like, pick up any copy of *House Beautiful* magazine, and you'll immediately see.

PART TWO
RISING SIGNS

WHAT IS A **RISING** SIGN?

Your rising sign is the zodiacal sign that could be seen rising on the eastern horizon at the time and place of your birth. Each sign takes about two and a half hours to rise — approximately one degree every four minutes. Because it is so fast moving, the rising sign represents a very personal part of the horoscope, so even if two people were born on the same day and year as one another, their different rising signs will make them very different people.

It is easier to understand the rising sign when the entire birth chart is seen as a circular map of the heavens. Imagine the rising sign — or ascendant — at the eastern point of the circle. Opposite is where the Sun sets — the descendant. The top of the chart is the part of the sky that is above, where the Sun reaches at midday, and the bottom of the chart is below, where the Sun would be at midnight. These four points divide the circle, or birth chart, into four. Those quadrants are then each divided into three, making a total of twelve, known as houses, each of which represents a certain aspect of life. Your rising sign corresponds to the first house and establishes which sign of the zodiac occupied each of the other eleven houses when you were born.

All of which makes people astrologically different from one another; not all Taureans are alike! The rising sign generally indicates what a person looks like. For instance, people with Leo, the sign of kings, rising, probably walk with a noble air and find that people often treat them like royalty. Those that have Pisces rising frequently have soft and sensitive looks and they might find that people are forever pouring their hearts out to them.

The rising sign is a very important part of the entire birth chart and should be considered in combination with the Sun sign and all the other planets!

THE RISING SIGNS FOR TAURUS

To work out your rising sign, you need to know your exact time of birth— if hospital records aren't available, try asking your family and friends. Now turn to the charts on pages 38–43. There are three charts, covering New York, Sydney, and London, all set to Greenwich Mean Time. Choose the correct chart for your place of birth and, if necessary, add or subtract the number of hours difference from GMT (for example, Sydney is approximately ten hours ahead, so you need to subtract ten hours from your time of birth). Then use a ruler to carefully find the point where your GMT time of birth meets your date of birth—this point indicates your rising sign.

TAURUS WITH ARIES RISING

These energetic and competitive Taureans are not all they seem. You might be forgiven for thinking that they are rash and foolhardy but, in fact, each and every one of their lightning-fast decisions or actions has a purpose, and usually it's a material one. The person with the Sun in Taurus and Aries rising is energetic and tends to reach out to people with a childlike appeal. Self-confident and optimistic, they'll stroll through life because they know how to attract the good things. Possessions are important to them and can sometimes serve as a measure of who they are. If this sense of themselves doesn't fluctuate too much, they will feel safe but they need to learn to value themselves for their many qualities. They have a daring streak that doesn't always show. If there is someone or something that strikes their fancy, they won't hesitate to pursue that person or track the object down. When their passions are fired up, they'll go for what they desire—no holds barred!

TAURUS WiTH **TAURUS** RiSiNG

This Taurus is naturally commanding and laid-back at the same time, with a big dose of self-confidence that could be mistaken for arrogance and upset those with less self-esteem. They are magnanimous, loving, and sensual, with a warm aura, but any attempts to persuade them to do anything that they don't want to do will be in vain! They will charmingly carry on with what they believe should be done and, infuriatingly, they are rarely wrong! However, the "double" Taurus is honest and trustworthy to a fault. They may be unmovable but anyone who follows this Bull's path will be able to share in their many favors and rich rewards because this is not only a very lucky Bull, but also a very generous one. These Taureans are very popular; their faces are as bright as stars and light seems to emanate from their very hearts, so others are often attracted to them.

TAURUS WiTH **GEMiNi** RiSiNG

Ⅱ Taurus with Gemini rising comes across as happy-go-lucky and easygoing, but this isn't the entire picture. A Taurus is a Taurus— down-to-earth, practical, and laid-back but stubborn—but with Gemini rising, there's a slightly different message to be found. They will try hard to impress by putting on a front that says, "I'm ready, willing, and able to blend in and do as you like," but this is not what they really mean. They would prefer others to meld into their world and do as they like, but in order to draw them into their mindset, they will first give the impression that they are willing to be what others want. Confusing? The more familiar you are with this person, the more confusing it gets, but this makes them no less lovable. Anyway, everyone manipulates, and the fact is that this Taurus is eager to love and has a huge capacity for giving. They just need to be made to feel safe. They are clever, quick-witted, and good at handling cash. They need lots of reassurance and, with the right people, they will be the typical loyal, warm, and luscious Taureans that deep down inside, they really are.

TAURUS WiTH **CANCER** RiSiNG

♋ Cancer adds some extra comfort, warmth, and security, so the Taurus with Cancer rising knows just how to nurture, protect, and provide, whether materially or spiritually. Put simply, they know how to make others feel good. They are the ultimate clan-leaders—calm, gentle, and loving, with a strong sense of purpose and a good dose of tenacity. They have an amazing way with people and are constantly attuned to the crowd's needs. They are friendly and sociable, and others are naturally drawn to them, not only because they make the best party food, but also because there's a special soothing quality about them that makes people feel at ease and free to be themselves. Being deeply loyal, the person with the Sun in Taurus and with Cancer rising cannot bear insincerity and does not forgive easily when slighted by others. They demand allegiance from close friends and family alike but give it back in return. As long as everyone in their circle gets on together, they are happy for anyone to remain there, and, as they are incredibly sensitive, picking up a vibe is old hat for these Taureans. In a nutshell, they are warm and embracing.

TAURUS WITH **LEO** ☉ RISING

♌ The Taurus with Leo rising is the one who aspires to being "King of the Castle" but it takes a long time to get to that point, so the period of adjustment could cause some friction early on. They know what they want and are incredibly determined and ambitious, yet also trustworthy and dependable. The person with the Sun in Taurus and Leo rising is fantastic to have in a labor force because they will work tirelessly toward a goal until they reach the top, which is where they know they belong. However, once comfortably seated in a position of control, don't try to move them—this is one bossy Taurus with a ferocious temper! As long as others do as they say and carry out their wishes, they'll be as sweet as anything. They aren't as difficult to handle as they sound, especially not for someone who is equally demanding. With their regal looks and love of luxury, they're usually the ones to provide the luxury, and they don't mind others mooching off them because it makes them feel charitable—which they are. They're also unbendingly honorable, altruistic, and admirable.

TAURUS WITH **VIRGO** RISING

Earthy and earnest, practical and sensible, yet the Taurus with Virgo rising still manages to be sensual and tender, even passionate. However, this isn't necessarily immediately apparent. In fact, it might take a while to draw these Taureans out because they tend toward shyness, or at least it appears that way. They make little noise and won't openly object to very much, so you might assume that they harbor some deep inner secret. The truth is that, although they will let you know if something doesn't meet with their approval, they are simply easygoing creatures who usually wear their hearts on their sleeve. Okay, so they can also be particular, and when they're particular, they're really particular! But it's nothing to worry about; just abide by their wishes and everything will be fine. They mean well and they're authentic; there's nothing to hide here! Just remember, too, that they're never likely to be caught in a fix. The Taurus with Virgo rising is someone who plans ahead down to the very last detail. Their motto is "Be Prepared"—Scout's honor!

TAURUS WiTH **LiBRA** RisinG

These deeply sweet and determined romantics have the energy of Venus, goddess of love, oozing out of all their pores. They can't help having the kind of appeal that makes others want to get "up close and personal." However, while on the surface they couldn't be more charming and attentive, Taureans with Libra rising are highly selective when it comes to allowing others into their space. They're idealistic and have a finely tuned sense of discernment, which means they'll settle for nothing less than the profoundly deep and meaningful. That goes for every activity they engage in, whether it's work, rest, or play. This is an incredibly creative combination and those who possess it have a hidden intensity that often displays itself in their commitment to an artistic pursuit. Taureans with Libra rising are also adept at discovering what makes others tick, knowing instinctively how to bring out the best (and worst!) in every individual they meet. They know all the right (and wrong!) buttons to push. Their desire for love, beauty, and luxury is a powerful driving force, although most people would be surprised how deep this desire runs, so great is their outward calm and laid-back manner.

TAURUS WiTH **SCORPiO** RisinG

Taureans with Scorpio rising are a reserved but powerful force of nature, so strong and tenacious that nothing they put their mind to is left incomplete. They conduct their life's business with a quiet, even secretive, determination, possessing a talent for shrewd and subtle handling of commercial affairs. They have a keen insight into others, who often feel that they are being weighed and measured under Taurus' scrutiny. This, along with their outward self-control, allows them always to be one step ahead in a partnership, whether of a business or personal nature. They show no fear when expressing their desires and demands and are deeply sensual creatures with a possessive and jealous streak when it comes to romantic attachments. They are staunchly loyal and protective toward those they form a personal commitment with, offering constant support and security, both materially and emotionally. However, their brusque and blunt manner can make them appear unapproachable and it's impossible for anyone other than their nearest and dearest to try to impose on them. Behind the gritty, stubborn exterior, they have a sweet sensitivity and soft vulnerability that are true treasures, and they guard them with all their strength of will.

TAURUS WITH **SAGITTARIUS** RISING

When Sagittarius is rising, Taurus takes on a more outgoing personality, becoming the "bon viveur", who enjoys all that life has to offer, and who is spontaneous and adventurous. There's a touch of the dinner-party animal about them: they adore spending time in the company of interesting characters with whom, over a table groaning with delectable dishes, they can eat, drink, and solve the problems of the world. But this is no superficial pastime; they genuinely mean well and truly wish to embrace uplifting and worthy causes. While retaining the persistence and hard-working side of their Sun sign, they focus their attention on being of help to others, performing charitable deeds, and lending their considerable strength and support to the people and causes they believe in. However, the Taurus with Sagittarius rising is no slavish, self-sacrificing doormat. They're unlikely to allow others to take advantage of their good nature, but when called upon to lend a hand with something they deem important, they will regularly perform above and beyond the call of duty. They are also extremely well accomplished when it comes to business affairs and are quick to see the potential in something and take advantage of any opportunity that offers solid, material gain. Their steady good humor and generous approach to life make them very popular individuals.

TAURUS WiTH **CAPRiCORN** RiSiNG

Those people born with the Sun in Taurus while Capricorn was rising, are serious, cautious, and very self-reliant. This combination matches determination with ambition. They want to reach great heights and tenaciously set out to get there, allowing little to get in their way as they journey ever upward. They appear so quiet, contemplative, outwardly content, and satisfied, that no one would ever guess the amount of effort they expend diligently searching for just the right path to follow and the best way to get their foot onto the next rung of the ladder. As a result, they often end up very wealthy. They use the same approach in the personal relationships they form and won't waste time on flippant, flirtatious fancies, preferring to move a partnership on step by solid step. The Taurus with Capricorn rising has a hidden but surprisingly romantic side and an intense desire to get deeply and physically involved. Once they've become attached, they find it very difficult to let go if things go wrong as they're loath to write off all the time, effort, and feelings they've invested in what proved to be a wasted enterprise. Creativity is another, less obvious trait, but Taureans with Capricorn rising have the patience needed to become true masters of the arts. They take themselves very seriously and so should everyone else.

TAURUS WITH **AQUARIUS** RISING

〰〰 This combination makes a "know all" and, unfortunately for others, 〰〰 they do know it all and, what's more, they're going to tell everyone! The Taurus with Aquarius rising has an incredible memory for facts, excellent and logical reasoning skills, and a practical, honorable disposition. Outwardly they're friendly and sincere, and it's difficult to resist their powerful presence, but although they appear so pleasant, pity the person who disagrees with them. Taureans with Aquarius rising will brook no opposition and will set out determinedly to enlighten that foolish opponent, no matter how long it takes. Usually very sociable, they adore being in the company of friends, especially those with whom they share some connection. They would feel unsettled and terribly insecure if they weren't attached to a brother- or sisterhood of like-minded individuals all pursuing the same goal—that is, world domination, and peace and happiness for all (in that order!) This person also loves presents, preferably receiving rather than giving, although they can be very generous. Any token of friendship or love that they've received will be treasured and put proudly on display, whatever its material worth or attractiveness: its presence speaks of acceptance and security.

TAURUS WITH **PISCES** RISING

Taurus with Pisces rising is a sympathetic character indeed, exuding a quiet and modest loving kindness but with a powerful core that attracts others with the sense of comfort and security that it appears to offer. This lovely person has a natural ability to key into the emotional depths of all those around them. They understand almost telepathically what's going on in their heart of hearts, so much so that these sweet and courteous Taureans often need to erect barriers between themselves and others and not be so impressionable and receptive. They can take on others' feelings so easily that they don't know where they end and the other person begins. Although they are very trusting, gentle, and affable, they also have a keen ability to spot a fraud. They don't take kindly to attempts to pull the wool over their eyes and will quickly withdraw and stubbornly maintain their distance from anyone false or deceptive. They have a profound love of music, poetry, and art, often displaying an exceptional ability to communicate through these mediums. Whether they are inspired by the arts or are inspiring others through them, people should listen closely to what they have to say.

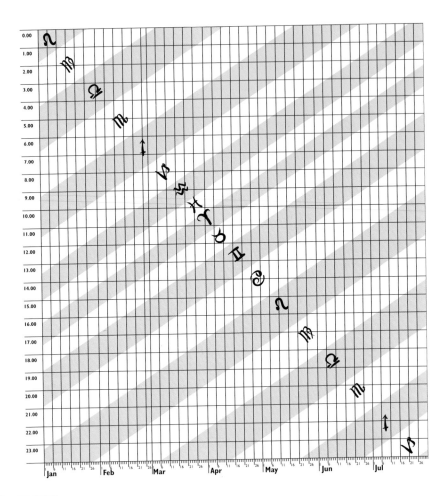

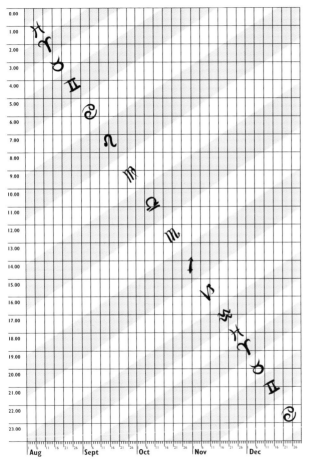

RISING SIGN
CHART

New York

latitude 39N00
meridian 75W00

♈ aries	♎ libra
♉ taurus	♏ scorpio
♊ gemini	♐ sagittarius
♋ cancer	♑ capricorn
♌ leo	♒ aquarius
♍ virgo	♓ pisces

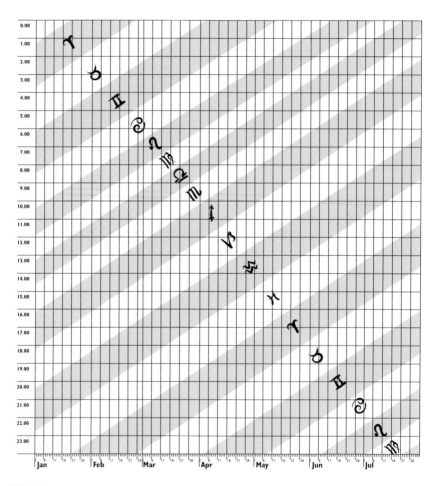

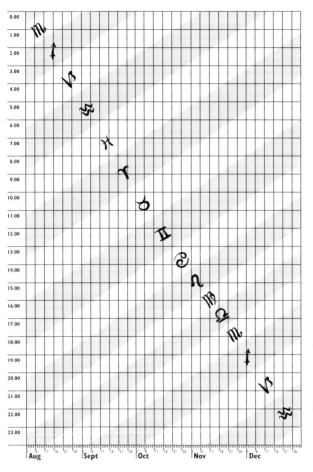

RISING SIGN
CHART

Sydney

latitude 34S00
meridian 150E00

♈	aries	♎	libra
♉	taurus	♏	scorpio
♊	gemini	♐	sagittarius
♋	cancer	♑	capricorn
♌	leo	♒	aquarius
♍	virgo	♓	pisces

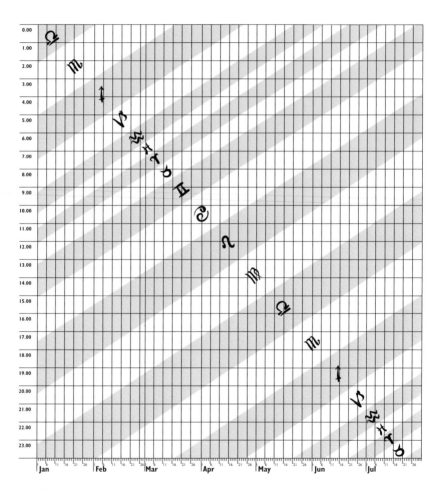

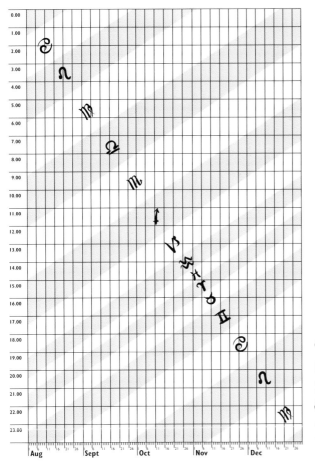

♈ aries		♎ libra	
♉ taurus		♏ scorpio	
♊ gemini		♐ sagittarius	
♋ cancer		♑ capricorn	
♌ leo		♒ aquarius	
♍ virgo		♓ pisces	

PART THREE
RELATIONSHIPS

THE **TAURUS** FRIEND

The steadfast, loyal, and laid-back nature of Taurus individuals makes them comforting, easygoing friends. They like to take their time getting to know somebody, so they'll never reject anyone outright at the first meeting. Even if they find nothing in common with a new acquaintance, they won't put up any barriers to their friendship but will instead simply focus their attention on others whom they feel they get on with better. When Taureans have decided to include someone in their close circle of friends, it would take a herd of wild elephants to come between them, and sometimes not even then!

Once the bond of friendship has been forged, it requires some pretty terrible behavior on the part of the other person to make Taureans sever all ties completely. But once they do, they'll stubbornly stick to their decision in the same way that they stubbornly stick by their friends through good times and bad. Taureans are never fair-weather friends. It makes no difference to them whether it's been two hours or two years since the last meeting; they just pick up where they left off and ask, "What's new?"

Taureans have fixed ideas and opinions so it can be difficult to make them change their minds but they're just as happy to admit when they know nothing about a subject and then, since patience is one of their virtues, they'll simply let others have their say. A Taurus friend is a friend for life!

TAURUS WiTH **ARiES**

Aries is naturally drawn to the kindness and understanding that seems to ooze from the pores of Taurus. Taurus can't help but be curious and entertained by the lively energy of Aries. Although Aries will be straight in there with a smile, forming a friendship without a second's hesitation, Taurus is a little more cautious, at least in the beginning. Taurus likes to pace the journey while Aries runs on full throttle. But both indulge passionately in whatever interests them and if they find a subject that is mutually intriguing, then this is the perfect combination for developing a lasting, loyal bond and friendship. Sometimes exciting, always steady.

TAURUS WiTH **TAURUS**

Put simply, there are other signs more suited to friendship with a Taurus than another Taurus. It's not that they're difficult people. On the contrary, Taurus is sensitive, understanding, loyal, calm, and affectionate, but can be incredibly obstinate and territorial. So, should there be a disagreement between them or some overstepping of the boundaries, the result may be an explosion of temper followed by long periods of sulking and silence. With so much shared stubbornness, they could end up waving red rags at one another far too often.

TAURUS WiTH GEMiNi

Taurus's earthy approach can help to ground the airy nature of Gemini, so in this respect they're very good for one another. Gemini's agile, intellectual approach will add another dimension to the Taurus tendency to think only in concrete terms. Taurus can offer the advantages of stability and security, while Gemini provides the fascination of bright, new, and lively conversation. After a while, however, Gemini's flippant behavior and inability to stay still could irritate the Bull, but Gemini's quick thinking usually comes to the rescue before there's any major problem.

TAURUS WiTH CANCER

Taurus is honest and won't mess with this sensitive Cancer friend and Cancer intuitively knows how to support the needs of Taurus and will effortlessly offer understanding. There are some similarities between them so they may feel a certain familiarity with one another. Both are sensitive, emotional, and caring, yet they both know how to have a great time. In many ways they are a reflection of one another so they feel a natural rapport. However, Cancer can, on occasion, be changeable, unpredictable, and grumpy, which could destabilize the Bull, who demands constancy and an emotionally safe environment.

TAURUS WITH **LEO**

Unless there's the deep bond between them that comes from a shared experience, this may be a difficult friendship to maintain. Taurus will naturally be vulnerable to the charm and grace of Leo and will find Leo's warmth and generosity very appealing. Leo, meanwhile, admires the strength and delightfully indulgent tendency of Taurus. However, Taurus can do without the demands and high drama of the Leo personality, while Leo would probably appreciate a little more spontaneity than Taurus can offer. At worst, arguments could get nasty and since neither takes well to being proved wrong, a battle of wills is often the result. Take one day at a time.

TAURUS WITH **VIRGO**

Being a Mercurial sign, Virgo, with its witty remarks, insightfulness, and ability to reason things through with precision, will never fail to hold the Bull's interest. Taurus, meanwhile, offers unwavering calm and loyal and steadfast support that can soothe and calm Virgo friends whenever they are nervous or on edge. However, Taureans don't enjoy having their Virgo friends over-analyze their psychology, and their famous stubbornness is very limiting to Virgo's quick and nimble mind. However, as both signs are of the Earth element, there is a good rapport between them and the relationship flows easily, with each having a very grounded and natural understanding of the other.

TAURUS WiTH **LiBRA**

Since both are ruled by the planet Venus, these two form the original mutual admiration society. They share a love of all things beautiful. Having said that, Libra enjoys the conceptual idea of beauty while Taurus needs to experience it in a concrete manner. When Taurus gets angry and sees a red rag waving, or gets too rigid and opinionated, Libra will have to rely heavily on the sign's diplomatic skills. In turn, it can be difficult for Taurus, who likes to have a plan to stick to, to pin down and put up with the indecisive Libra. All in all, though, these two appreciate each other and couldn't want for a friend with more interests in common.

TAURUS WiTH **SCORPiO**

Scorpio feels deep affection and respect for Taurus, while Taurus will be patient and understanding, even when Scorpio is in one of the sign's darker moods. These two signs are opposite one another in the zodiac, which means that there are similarities between them. For example, both can be very stubborn so stand-offs and power struggles could be the result. Taurus is very down-to-earth but will be fascinated by Scorpio, who goes much deeper than that. They'll either be so taken with one another that they can't imagine life without the other, or be so repulsed that they can't imagine life with the other. But the solution will soon become apparent and they won't have a problem agreeing on it.

TAURUS WiTH **SAGiTTARiUS**

Sagittarius is never short of bright ideas. This intrigues Taurus to begin with, but when Taurus really wishes to follow up one of the ideas, Sagittarius is unlikely to treat it seriously and this will annoy Taurus, who doesn't take too well to flippancy. These two signs could both respond to a new plan with equal amounts of passion, but then they'll proceed in different ways. They might end up having a very productive relationship and working in tandem, but generally speaking, there's little common ground between them. Sagittarius is a wide-ranging traveler, while Taurus is most comfortable at home or kicking back and relaxing. However, in small doses, this friendship could work well.

TAURUS WiTH **CAPRiCORN**

These two Earth signs have so much in common and so much they can do together. Both are grounded types of people, who can help, encourage, and advise one another, whether it's on the subject of making a sound investment or tackling some home decorating. They make the perfect pair and friendship will readily blossom between them. However, they sometimes feel that the outside world infringes on the time that they want to spend together, so they run the risk of shutting everyone else out. Both are realists, which leaves little room for imaginative horseplay, but who cares? As long as the chores are finished, all that's left to do is unwind and chill out!

TAURUS WiTH **AQUARiUS**

Taurus is practical and business-minded and Aquarius is innovative. Got the picture? As business partners, these two could end up seriously rich simply by putting their heads together. However, as friends, Aquarius might have a problem with Taurus's inability to act on the spur of the moment, and Taurus might find it hard to appreciate some of Aquarius's finer qualities, such as the love of freedom. Aquarius won't like the idea of being Taurus's best or soul—especially sole—mate. Aquarius likes to have plenty of friends. However, since both have a tendency to take up rather fixed positions, they had better enjoy getting into frequent not-so-friendly debates if this friendship is to last!

TAURUS WiTH **PiSCES**

Taurus can be a little stubborn, rigid, and opinionated, while the flowing intellect of Pisces shows no bounds. This is a discrepancy that can cause a few problems but nothing that can't be overcome. Pisces is usually happy to go along with what Taurus suggests because the Bull has a real ability to make the Fish feel comfortable and happy. They have similar needs and wants in the sense that both like to find the easy route in most situations and both appreciate peace and quiet. Pisces's mutability helps to break down the inflexibility that Taurus is known for, so, they'll naturally seek out the middle ground and reach the perfect agreement.

THE **TAURUS WOMAN** IN LOVE

This very sensual, feminine woman was born under a sign that's ruled by amorous Venus—the planet of love. The Taurus woman in love is unstoppable, adoring, supportive, and, above all else, genuine. This should be every man's dream-come-true but some men, particularly those who are prone to getting cold feet in a relationship, find it a little overbearing. If this is the case, it is best either to explore whether there is scope for certainty and commitment or opt out straight away. Taurus's very real and natural sexuality is a serious attraction but it's not to be toyed with. Her favors will only be granted to those who have earned them and, if her partner proves disloyal, her intense possessiveness comes into play and she won't hesitate to demonstrate her ragingly bullish side.

The Taurus woman knows how to indulge herself but, even more, she will totally spoil and pamper her man, especially if he has offered himself entirely to her. Her earthly senses are particularly finely tuned. She loves the sight and scent of fresh flowers, she melts over a cordon-bleu meal, she'll get misty-eyed at the sound of beautiful music, and, best of all, she loves the subtle feel of silky lingerie—which she knows how to wear and how to remove! Although she is very accepting, the Taurus woman can't help but be put off by vulgarity such as bad odor, offensive sights and sounds, or crass behavior! She won't reject a man with bad habits but she'll expect him to play up to her many desires and to tickle her delicate senses.

This is a woman who'll give all she's got to keep her man happy, just as long as he's devoted to her. She has the patience of a saint but, push her too far on the loyalty front, and she'll let her man know her feelings with a ferocity that only a Leo can match. However, the Taurus woman is dignified, courageous, and full of commonsense. She is honest and loyal beyond question, and with all these positive characteristics, it's not surprising that many men fall at her feet. But she is not one to play games. On the contrary, she is straightforward and knows what she wants!

Typically, she has a mind of her own and is self-controlled: she's not the type who will fly off the handle at the slightest irritation. It takes a lot to make her lose her restraint, except in bed, which is great for the man. She celebrates a man's masculinity and makes him feel like a real man. He can rely on her and share everything with her without having to worry that she'll storm off with his money or, worse, with another man—unless, of course, he's behaved diabolically toward her. When this is the case, she'll make sure he gets a good tongue lashing. Perhaps, even, a good hiding.

TAURUS WOMAN WITH **ARIES MAN**

In love: He is the man of men. Being an Aries and ruled by Mars, he is positively and deliciously masculine, impulsive, and aggressive. He could be very protective toward the lady Bull, who, being an Earth sign ruled by the planet Venus, is the ultimate sensuously indulgent female. He'll be attracted to her immediately, without knowing why, but that won't bother him. He'll happily accept the peace and understanding that she offers. She'll be someone to wipe his weary brow and envelop him in emotional and physical luxury while he recharges his batteries. She, on the other hand, will find his boyish bravado irresistible. He brings such excitement and newness to her life. He's never boring, always active, and rarely gets under her feet. And that's where things might not always be perfect, for occasionally she likes having him around and one hundred percent there for her. She is possessive, and he doesn't take kindly to being tied down. He will always be there for her, as long as she doesn't demand his presence. In return, she will bring stability and security to his fast-paced lifestyle. The Taurus woman enjoys frequent quiet moments, when there's just the two of them together and a heavy scent of romance in the air. He, the ultimate masculine figure, will be drawn by her feminine charms and her offer of love and devotion. They might not recognize it immediately, but this couple has a lot to offer one another in the long term.

In bed: There's never a dull moment with the Aries man! He's full of surprises and this could either make the Taurus lady a little edgy or it could fill her with delightful anticipation, making her perpetually ready and willing to find out what's going to happen next. His enthusiasm can be infectious, especially if she's up for the thrills and spills that the Aries man never fails to provide. It will take time and patience on the part of the Taurus woman to get her Aries man to consider her sexual needs, since he can be a bit of a "wham-bam-thank-you-ma'am" kind of lover. She normally prefers a slower pace. But she shouldn't be too quick to judge. That's his department, being master of the quickie. Although this man might not give her all she needs first time around, he doesn't always stop with just one fleeting sexual session. When he's decided that he wants an evening of sex, he's a many-times-a-night-guy. The Taurus woman has both the stamina and the sensual allure to make sure she has her desires satisfied, and often! His raw energy is highly desirable but if she feels that he needs taming, she's certainly got the depth and the patience to do it. He may burst with eagerness while she slowly and thoroughly shows him her way, but given time, he'll learn to hold back. She'll show him what to do and he won't forget in a hurry because he'll quickly become addicted to her sensuous touch and will want to come back for more!

TAURUS WOMAN WITH **TAURUS MAN**

In love: When Taureans work, they throw themselves into it completely, which is why they are often successful in their careers and good with money. When they relax, they do it one hundred percent, which is why they have a reputation for being lazy. And so it is in love—all or nothing. Whenever they get the chance, they just want to immerse themselves in one another, which means they risk becoming permanent loungers who overuse home-delivery services for everything from food and wine to sex toys. Even so, they won't always be stuck on their backsides. Taurus is one of the most sensual signs. They know exactly how to seduce and satisfy one another, and this could last for days on end! They are truly romantic, buying each other tokens of love, declaring their undying loyalty, and exchanging the sort of sentimental cards that make most people cringe! The support that they give each other brings both of them an overwhelming sense of acceptance and security and, since they are equally possessive and jealous, there is an unspoken agreement between them that, when they are out together socially, they present a united front that nobody, not even the most determined flirt, could penetrate. Even though they're both stubborn and their silence-filled arguments can feel insoluble at times, they're generally so calm and relaxed that they won't end up at loggerheads very often. In its own way, this is a beautiful match, with a love that will last longer than any disagreement.

In bed: These two lovers both wanna get physical and, for them, anything earthy and natural goes. Since they're total realists, they don't need to dress up in fancy clothes, though they do appreciate seductive silk nightwear. But it all ends up coming off anyway, which gives them the chance to really look at and appreciate one another's bodies. This relationship is pure physicality and it is scandalously stimulating. They take their time at everything and that includes romantic lovemaking. Talk about stamina! Who said these guys were lazy? They use all the determination of a long-distance runner to reach a state of physical bliss. Lovemaking between the Taurus man and the Taurus woman is dizzying and ecstatic. They certainly don't need drugs, although they'll probably enjoy a mid-session feast of oysters, chocolate, and champagne, and once they've finished dining on the bed, they'll carry on dining on each other. Its hedonistic heaven! Their earth will move until they are both deliciously exhausted, and then they'll hold each other close until the light of day. It could be either of them who gets up to make breakfast in bed, but whichever one it is, breakfast's sure to be served with a rose and a kiss. Actions speak louder than words.

TAURUS WOMAN WITH GEMINI MAN

In love: This is not an impossible love match, but a Taurus woman will probably expect a lot more from her partner than a Gemini man can give. Gemini and Taurus appear to be like chalk and cheese, but these two signs are next to one another in the zodiac, which indicates that they could have more in common than meets the eye. If there is a spark between them, it will be very special indeed. The Taurus woman's earthy approach can help to ground the airy nature of the Gemini man, and the Gemini man's whimsical cheerfulness will no doubt introduce some new and exciting elements to the Taurus woman's life. He's impressed by her sense of beauty and creativity, and she delights in his witty conversation. The Gemini man's constant flow of ideas will always add a fresh dimension to the Taurus woman's tendency to think in concrete terms. In this respect they are good for one another and they make a colorful, dynamic couple. The question is: Will the Taurus woman's patience eventually wear thin when all she wants to do is relax, while Gemini man wants to satisfy his untiring thirst for new people, places, and things? In Gemini talk, the answer is "yes" or, perhaps, "no." With Gemini, things can chop and change unless they have a pact between them. In the language of a Taurus, this means "commitment," but that's a word that could be interpreted in a myriad of ways by the Gemini man.

In bed: The Gemini man certainly knows a thing or two about variety and if he can apply this to his Taurus woman, then she'll make him feel more than man enough in return. Meanwhile, the Taurus woman could probably teach any Tantric sex practitioner a few things about endurance and holding back. When she applies this knowledge to her Gemini man, she can bring him to a truly intense level of toe-curling ecstasy. Between the sheets, on the dining-room table, or out in the yard in the open air, the Taurus woman has a lot to offer the Gemini man, and if she can hold his attention for long enough, he'll be immensely grateful for the earth-moving pleasure that she gives. He needs as much mental stimulation as physical to get him vibrating at the right frequency to give her sexual pleasure. On the other hand, the Gemini man will appeal to the Taurus woman's imagination, allowing her to lie back while he gets her going with his fantastic tales of love and lust. However, he's such a social butterfly that when he flutters around a room chatting with whichever pretty thing catches his attention, it's likely to be her jealousy rather than her passion that he arouses. If their romance is still intact once the reality of his flirtatious behavior meets her intransigent possessive streak, they'll both end up glowing with smug pride.

TAURUS WOMAN WITH CANCER MAN

In love: When the Taurus woman gets together with the Cancer man, romantic Venus meets protective Moon and both planets shine out in the heavenly night skies, radiating a sense of warmth and security. This is exactly what these two lovers do for each other. Their cozy coupling is based on emotional and physical accord. Add that to their mutual love of comfort and luxury, and the result is a glowing combination. They share the same ideals and both have a sixth sense about how to enhance each other's natural ability to bring in the money that will buy their own perfect piece of paradise. Two people who are so much on the same wavelength can't help but be in love. There is a playful friendship between them and acceptance of each other's foibles, so when they get together, problems just seem to fade away. Both are sensitive and emotional. She revels in the romantic; he's receptive and responsive. In many ways they're a reflection of one another, each feeling a deep sense of empathy with the other. He, however, can be changeable and grumpy, needing to protect himself from the constant barrage of emotions that assault him from the outside world. This can destabilize the Lady Bull, who demands constancy and dislikes being emotionally relegated, although with her natural patience and determination to see things through, once he changes back again, it doesn't take long for them to pick up from where they left off. In fact, her stubbornness could easily be the cause of this "crabby" man's retreat into his shell, but it's also one of the qualities he finds most attractive in her since he needs a strong sense of security in order to show off his talents. Once in each other's hearts, they will have a fine romance that they'll find it difficult to get out of.

 In bed: This is a mesmerizing experience for them both. They could get so seriously lost in one another that they forget simple little things like the time of day. However, one thing that won't be forgotten is mealtimes. They're both big food-lovers, so their lovemaking may well include some gastronomic specialties to heighten the delicious effect, while her supreme sensuality will never fail to feed the Cancer man's ravenous hunger for her body. The Taurus lady may be a little clumsy at first, as she takes charge of her strong physical desires and attunes them to her Cancer lover, but meanwhile, he'll go with the flow, reaching her most sensitive zones—and she has lots of those. This is a very sexy lady who adores the feeling of physical closeness and gives her body over completely to the experience of making love. Whatever the mood of her Cancer man, she'll succeed in exciting him and he'll make his enjoyment of giving her physical pleasure very obvious, which suits the Taurus woman just fine, because nothing turns her on more. This is the ultimate bedroom encounter, with one player as adoring as the other. She will never fail to fulfill his physical needs and he will fulfill hers as often as she likes!

TAURUS WOMAN WiTH **LEO MAN**

 In love: Tempestuous though this combination can be, these Sun signs have certain things in common that could keep them together for a very long time, if not forever—namely, loyalty and affection. These are the basic needs of the Lion, and the Taurus woman will be there to provide him with them on a permanent basis. She doesn't give her heart away lightly so, when she finally does, she expects it to be for keeps, and the same goes for him. Although the Leo man appears fierce, he is much more sensitive than he wants people to think. His pride is easily hurt and he will reward the Taurus woman's ability to offer steadfast love and appreciation with the most generous and warm-hearted tenderness and devotion—all of which will delight the Lady Bull. She enjoys an expensive, indulgent lifestyle, but the showy flamboyance and impractical ostentation that the Leo man finds thrilling could stretch their purse strings beyond even her forbearance. Nor will he enjoy having to curb his playfulness to suit her need for a man with a sense of purpose and responsibility. He can be as responsible as the next guy. He just has his own unique and individual way of showing it. The key to avoiding difficulties in this relationship is for both to be aware of the other's strong will. If they give each other a wide berth to make space for their difference, their love could go far. Disregard the superficial differences, and there is the potential for something deep.

 In bed: The raw sexual energy of the Leo man is something for the sensually sexual Taurus woman to reckon with. It truly makes her quiver with anticipation, the way he prowls around her with that gleam of erotic hunger in his eye. It drives her mad with desire as she waits for this male Lion to pounce. She will play up to his nobility and whisper the most seductively complimentary words in his ear, and he'll repay her tenfold. Leo is a regal sign, after all. He'll smile, or purr, at being recognized for the king that he is and he'll never treat his partner as anything less than a queen. Sure, he may occasionally require her to bow down in front of him but the Taurus lady will happily comply. He will never give her any reason to feel possessive or insecure and she will know that he is, and always will be, hers. If there's any playing around, it will only be behind closed doors and between the two of them, and what a delightful romp that will be.

TAURUS WOMAN WITH **VIRGO MAN**

In love: Since both the Taurus woman and the Virgo man are rather cautious, it would be unusual to find these two in bed together by the end of their first date. They are much more likely to spend their time finding out if they have any interests in common. Once they get beyond their initial reticence—particularly the reticence of the Virgo man—there will be some very sultry signals sent out. It won't take too long for them to grow really fond of one another and build a very solid foundation of love. Born under the sign of the Virgin, the Virgo man's innocence appeals to the Taurus woman, but make no mistake, he's not that innocent. The Virgo man is really much more knowing about what makes people tick and what captures their hearts than he lets on. Both of these players have a peaceful disposition, which is always an inducement to love. The Virgo man offers intelligent conversation, while the Taurus woman gives him the tranquility and understanding he needs. She may get a little sore at his finicky, fastidious ways, and by the fact that he occasionally criticizes everything from her choice of home decoration to her deodorant. In turn, he may take exception to her self-indulgent lazing around in front of the television when it's her turn to do the dishes. But with both of them being Earth signs, they have a natural affinity. They'll not only like one other: given the chance, they'll adore one another, too.

In bed: The passionate Virgo man has hidden depths, but he'll be far more interested in finding hers. This will certainly raise his interest and, being the helpful sort, he'll always be willing to lend a hand! Virgos are known for their skillful manual dexterity and the Taurus woman need not be shy about making use of his craftsmanship. She'll also find that he's very good at following instructions. She's so sexy that just the touch of her makes his heart beat faster, but her powerful sensuality will calm his nerves, massage away any tension, and help to ease him into a gentle rhythm. Seriously, these two are real earth-movers, and since that always requires a slow start, foreplay is definitely on their sexual menu. Speaking of menus, only the tastiest and most delectable morsels will do. And since she does require her man to have stamina, she will happily provide him with plenty of delicious treats, fed lovingly from her own hand, to help him keep his strength up. Once the Taurus woman and Virgo man are both intoxicated with the foods of love—consumed slowly, with every mouthful savored—they'll be ready to indulge each other in the extreme. Both can relish this moving experience.

TAURUS WOMAN WiTH LiBRA MAN

In love: Venus, the planet of love, rules both Taurus and Libra, but each sign approaches love in a different way. Her approach is mental, his is physical. And the odds are against them because the elements of Earth (her) and Air (him) are not normally compatible, but with

Venus uniting them, these problems can be transcended. Whatever happens, their ultimate aim is the same—love in its purest sense. If the Taurus woman and Libra man manage to achieve this, they'll find that the bond between them is as if sealed with a kiss from Aphrodite herself. What better blessing could there be? Their hearts can fly on the wings of love. However, it has to be said that the Libra man is a notorious flirt; he adores engaging women in scintillating conversation and delights in seeing the effect his charm has on them being reflected back at him from their eyes. This is very likely to cause the love he shares with Taurus to fly far away unless it gets the grounding that the Taurus woman can instill into the relationship. She's jealous and possessive, but much too controlled to fly into a rage. What is more likely to happen is that because she's hurt and confused by his behavior, she'll erect a wall between them to protect her vulnerability. Unless he's able to break it down quickly, he may find that wall getting so high and impenetrable that not even Aphrodite, the goddess of love, can bring about its destruction.

 In bed: Soft, sensuous, and romantic, the bedroom experience between the Taurus woman and Libra man will be like something from a storybook—or perhaps more like an erotic novel. It will be a tasteful treat in more ways than one. These Venus-ruled signs are into quality. From the atmospheric décor and scented candles to the carefully chosen fine champagne, this experience will appeal to the esthetic sense of them both. They really know how to enjoy themselves and, equally, how to please one another, despite their different approaches. The Taurus woman will enthuse the Libra man with her slow, steady movement, while the Libra man will excite the Taurus woman with his ability to move from one pleasure zone to another. They'll want to explore each other's forbidden fruits and will happily make a meal of it, but no knives and forks please—only bite-sized portions. The only problem facing this passionate pairing is his need for more than just a physical expression of togetherness. His intimacy must be one of the mind as well as the body. She, on the other hand, converses best through touch; her language is that of the caress. They may end up facing a communication breakdown that's impossible to fix.

TAURUS WOMAN WITH SCORPIO MAN

In love: Being an Earth sign, the Taurus woman will certainly enjoy having the Scorpio man as her excavation project. He's very deep and seemingly dark, but her senses inform her that it would be worth the effort of getting to the bottom of him. Once he gets used to her no-nonsense way of handling him, he'll not only be intrigued, he'll be hooked! He likes the way that she knows her own mind, is quietly in control of herself, and doesn't get flustered when he tries to probe her sensitive spots. This is one woman that the Scorpio man will not be able to play like a yo-yo. She won't even notice it if he attempts to manipulate her. She doesn't operate that way and never expects anyone else to, so it just passes over her like a wave on the seashore. The Scorpio man is after a deep and lasting intimacy and he needs a woman who will give herself to him fully, but until then he's happy to play around, so he may try to test her commitment during the formative stages of their relationship. But the Taurus woman is very matter-of-fact and, as a Bull, she certainly won't take any nonsense. The end-result will be that they'll never let each other down because they truly respect one another. Scorpio is ruled by Mars and Taurus by Venus—the cosmic lovers. That, plus the fact that the signs are opposite one another in the zodiac, means that there is an affinity binding them together like magnets. He is as hypnotic as she is alluring. Together they're a truly potent mixture.

In bed: The Taurus woman, being so deliciously indulgent and highly sensual, is a wonderfully rich lover. This suits the Scorpio man just fine, as he is intense, brooding, and always horny. He's perfect at handling her vast resources of sexual energy. This is one sizzling combination, and there is serious Tantric potential here! Patient as the Taurus woman is, however, when she gets it on with her Scorpio man, that patience flies right out of the window. Both are intensely passionate, but there's also mutual trust between them, which is just as well because their jealous rages are as intense as their sexual attractiveness. And since both are very aware of the destructive potential in their powerful emotions, it's unlikely they'll create any real trouble for each other with other partners, although it wouldn't be beyond the Scorpio man to try to spice up a party and arouse his Taurus lady's possessiveness with a hint of flirting. Once they get home to bed, though, they'll be as keen and eager as each other—but the Scorpio man won't want to let his Lady Bull know this too soon! He's a lover who's into teasing and titillating and he will be totally immersed in bringing his Taurus woman right to the edge. Luckily he doesn't believe in half-measures. He'll take her all the way.

TAURUS WOMAN WITH **SAGiTTARiUS MAN**

In love: The Taurus woman will find the Sagittarius man intriguing and esthetically pleasing, but this relationship will take some work. If she looks upon him as a project, she'll find her work cut out, and if she expects to slot into his life just like that, she'll be surprised to discover that it's not that easy. He will find her soothing manner comforting to come home to, but she will have to tolerate his need to be a free spirit. In other words, he won't come home very often. She'll find it impossible to rely on his time-keeping. He may say he'll be home at five, but that could mean five in the morning, or even in five days' time! Since she's a Fixed sign, she likes to make plans, but they all go out the window when she tries to make them with a Sagittarius man. One of their basic differences is that he finds it hard to relax and stay in one place, while she might find it hard to be spontaneous. These two are fundamentally different, but if they get past the first hurdle and the Taurus woman is not too offended by the wild Sagittarius man's wayward adventuring, lack of tact, and outspokenness, then love can develop. This is a union that will take time and effort to settle but if they give a little and are prepared to meet halfway, it could be an enlightening experience for both.

In bed: In a nutshell, the luxurious Taurus woman is expensive, while the adventurous Sagittarius man is expansive—which is not such a bad thing! For the Taurus woman, being in bed with a Sagittarius man is like being with someone from a completely different background and culture—he's like a foreigner in her land. It takes a bit of getting used to, but it can be very exotic. Once she sees how he glows when she parades around the bedroom in her brand new upmarket lingerie, it will be obvious that this holiday romance has serious potential. He's a lusty traveler who enjoys being on the move all over her body. He's also into learning, and if he has to spend all night studying every little bit of her, he'll happily do it—and he won't mind revising at regular intervals. She is as unembarrassed as he is when it comes to displays of physical desire, all of which he finds very sexy and appealing—shrinking violets are not his thing. However, should she ever try to tie him down for too long—even if it's with a pair of silk stockings to the bedstead—then his mind will start wandering, and with it his libido!

TAURUS WOMAN WITH CAPRICORN MAN

In love: Earthy, passionate, physical, and ambitious. These two lovers are on the same level and, what is more, they both want to go higher. The Taurus woman and Capricorn man understand each other superbly well, and the result is mutual trust and respect. What better foundation could there be for a long and lasting love? Since they're both totally absorbed in one another's aspirations, each is able to bring out the best in the other. Between them they have a mutual support system going. The sensuous Taurus lady is everything the Capricorn man could ever want in a woman. She's practical, sensible, and deliciously romantic. She thrills to his touch and offers him an abundance of affection. The Capricorn man is trustworthy and steady, serious when necessary, yet with a wonderfully ironic sense of humor that really tickles her fancy—all of which are major attractions for the Taurus woman. This is not a love that could ever be threatened by outside influences, no matter how tempting, so he's never going to feel vulnerable or she jealous. The Capricorn man might, at times, display a coolness that seems almost impenetrable, but her natural warmth and consistent tenderness will eventually break down any barriers. Their material aims are alike: both choose quality over quantity any day, so squabbles over money are non-existent. Because these two have such similar ideals, they are able to sense the divine spark in one another and their love could truly carry them into heaven.

 In bed: The Capricorn man is so understanding of the Taurus woman that she need never feel embarrassed about anything, and that includes her lusty, post-passion outpourings. He's seen it all before and, because he's so enamored of the Lady Bull, will gladly lap up everything she offers. His practicality means he has a waste-not want-not attitude! Bedroom manners? The Capricorn man is the perfect gentleman to his Taurus woman; he always says, "After you, m'lady," to which she always accedes with quivering grace. From the outside, this couple might look like Mr. and Mrs. Conventional, but once they're alone, they're anything but. There's a deliciously naughty side to their relationship, with him as a randy Goat and she enjoying the role of wood-nymph dancing to his pan-pipes. They love a pastoral frolic around the bedroom together. The intensity of their combined sexual energy is earth-shattering and they'll make the most of it. The only problem that these two have to tackle is, with all their worldly ambitions and activities, when do they ever find enough time to indulge their sensual appetites? What they always need to remember is that their powerful sexy bond is the glue holding their relationship together.

TAURUS WOMAN WiTH **AQUARiUS MAN**

In love: There are occasions when the Taurus lady will find interests in common with the Aquarius man, for instance, a mutual love and admiration for what the other is capable of. With his perceptive and friendly nature, the Aquarius man has much to offer her, especially in the way of keeping her up-to-date with modern thoughts and trends. However, his allergic reaction to anything remotely emotional and sentimental could bring this romantic and sensitive girl out in a bad case of weeping heart. For much as he adores her luxurious femininity and depth of understanding, even she will be hard-pressed to understand the manner in which he expresses it. The Aquarius man is detached from his emotions, although he often doesn't realize it. He is an admirable humanitarian at heart, but often forgets to nurture and adore those who are closest to him, while the Taurus woman will nurture and adore him and won't be able to comprehend why he doesn't return the compliment. If the Taurus woman can manage to find her own inner security while also cherishing the innumerable qualities of the Aquarius man, and if he can realize how good he feels bathed in her love and warmth, then he might just budge from his non-committal stance. This relationship grows slowly, but if the initial attraction retains a touch of sweetness, then it shouldn't be given up on too soon, though it will probably go through some bitter moments before it matures and ripens into a delicious, fruitful partnership.

 In bed: Everyone's got a bend, one way or another, but the Aquarius man is downright kinky; there isn't a sexual position in the book that he hasn't tried, although it would be fun to challenge him! That would certainly keep him interested, which is exactly what the Taurus lady needs to do if he is to indulge her desire for sensual fulfillment. However, if she has it her way, he'll occasionally need to stop intellectualizing and trying to figure out the latest Kama Sutra contortion, and will simply have to indulge in the physical process. Whether it's his way or her way, the delightful result will be that they're trying something new all the time. If she draws on her resources of patience, she'll get her fair share of bliss, but he'll probably have to struggle to maintain his need for innovation and she may be frustrated in her desire for emotional connection through lovemaking. Emotions get in the way of what he sees as the true meaning of love, so she could spend all evening listening to him discussing the abstract causes of love, rather than getting down to it. Sex is not the way to this man's heart. It's only the way into his trousers. He doesn't need physical affection to make him feel loved and wanted the way a Taurus girl does.

TAURUS WOMAN WiTH **PiSCES MAN**

In love: On the whole, the Taurus woman is level-headed and practical, and the Pisces man, although a very capable human being, is somewhat impractical and dreamy. The two seem like opposites at first, but in fact, they fit together like spoons. She will forget all her own practical aims once she mixes with the Fish; he helps her to float out of herself and this isn't such a bad thing. Where the Taurus woman has focus, the Pisces man looks at life through a prism, seeing the myriad possibilities in every situation. It would be easy for her to get drawn into his world and never come out of it, but would she really want to? For short spells of time, she's okay with that, and, in fact, finds it rather liberating and exciting. He provides a certain amount of romantic, emotional nourishment, but she's most comfortable on solid ground, which is where she really flourishes. Meanwhile, he'll benefit from her uncluttered vision and sense of direction: she can provide him with an elegant and comfortable container for the safe-keeping of his dreams. They each have strengths in areas where the other is lacking, and a mutual recognition of this fact makes for a pair of sympathetic lovers. Where this couple really align is in the realm of romance: their bodies and souls both feed on it. He will show her wonders and delights that capture her imagination just as she will arouse his physical senses with her intimate knowledge of pleasure. This is what binds them together and makes it difficult to pull them apart.

In bed: The problem for these two will be getting out of bed. For a Pisces man it's his number one domain—the place where he could live, eat, breathe, and work. He is an odd mixture of selfish and selfless, so if the Lady Taurus doesn't mind crumbs and beer cans littering the bed, he'll treat her to an unforgettable voyage from seduction to erogenous ecstasy. He has the sort of imagination that could make an ocean look shallow, so there will never be a dull moment in bed and he will happily spend hours on end in playful splashing. But the Pisces man is also sensitive, so when the Taurus woman has had enough and tells him so, he may feel hurt. However, this is unlikely to happen very often, because Lady Taurus has the stamina to outlast even the most ardent lover. What may cause her a few insecure moments, though, is his tendency to drift away on his own stream of dreams. She needs to feel her man up close and personal in every sense of the word. He tends not to verbalize but he needs his woman to do so with the sweetest, softest murmurs, which is something Lady Taurus knows how to do. She's not shy about expressing her needs and desires and this will encourage him to rise to the occasion and will make him more solid and dependable.

THE **TAURUS MAN** IN LOVE

The solid, earthy, and sensual Taurus man can put on a display of machismo without even thinking about it. He's very aware of the effect that this can have on a potential mate and because he enjoys having his vanity fanned, he'll only ever partner someone who responds with obvious delight to his powerful masculinity.

There's a hint of the chauvinist in him. He feels it's his due to be looked upon as the steadfast male protector of fragile femininity. He's very susceptible to elegance, glamor, and overt sexuality, but it may take him quite some time to decide whether or not to begin the process of wooing. Once he's set his mind to it, however, he'll throw himself into it like a bull at a gate. The Taurus man is just as practical and determined when he sets out to seduce a lover as he is with any other activity he tackles. His romantic nature and gentle touch, which somehow still manage to convey strength and constancy, could wear down even the most hardened heart. As a lover of luxury, indulgence, and beauty, he knows just how to provide the type of pleasure that excites the senses, whether it's a sumptuous candlelit meal or walking barefoot along a moonlit shore sharing a bottle of expensive champagne. The Taurus man is sure of himself and takes himself rather seriously, but when it comes to love, what he takes most seriously is his prowess in the bedroom. He is totally unabashed when it comes to his sexual appetites; there is absolutely no ambiguity in the way he expresses himself. He not only craves, but demands, a deep physical intimacy with his partner and has the stamina to spend all day and all night trying to achieve it. In the early stages of a romance he will frequently suggest spending an entire weekend at a hotel—one with an excellent room-service menu and a "do not disturb" sign to hang on the door—as an exercise in sexual bonding. It's probably the only exercise he really enjoys, since the Taurus man can be rather lazy. Unless the activity he is indulging in brings him enormous pleasure, he sees little point in it.

The Taurus man has a powerful possessive streak and sexual jealousy is deeply rooted in his nature. He will not put up with another man encroaching on his romantic territory and if he suspects his lover of fluttering her eyelashes at anyone other than him, then, like a wounded bull, he'll go charging in to devastating effect. Because he is so trustworthy in his devotion, he finds it hard to comprehend a faithless, fickle heart. His broad back can bear a heap of trouble, but should his lover be too lighthearted, fail to show enough affection, or cater insuficiently to his physical comfort, he can turn that back on her and stubbornly refuse to let her into his life. How things develop will depend on his lover. He will either stick to her or stick to his decision to shut her out. Either way, he sticks.

TAURUS MAN WITH **ARIES WOMAN**

 In love: Aries is attracted to almost anything with a pulse and the Taurus man's pulse is so strong and steady that if flashing lights were attached to him, the Aries lady would definitely be moving, grooving, and dancing to his beat! Romantically, the Taurus man will fulfill her deepest desires and offer a sense of emotional security, just as the energetic Aries lady inspires positive, pulsating action from her Bull. In order to keep this up, however, they will have to work hard. The Aries lady, coming home every day to a safe and secure environment, may find things somewhat monotonous and this may impel her to inject a new rhythm that could take him a while to get in step with. Fast on his feet this guy is not, but neither has he got two left ones. In fact, his grace of movement is deliciously appealing so long as the Aries girl doesn't fire up his temper, and then it's like putting "bull" and "china shop" together in the same life sentence. The first few weeks of this coupling should reveal all, and if they can get through the initial adjustments, they could very well go the whole distance. His calming influence on her is something that she could not only get used to, but also begin to enjoy, while the uplifting impact that the Aries female has on the Taurus man will undoubtedly make him feel more alive and keep him smiling.

 In bed: The Taurus man is romantic and will go to great lengths to set the mood with candles, fine wine, and luxurious surroundings. But the lady Ram may have to go against nature and slow down to enjoy the gradual build-up that the Taurus man loves to indulge in. The Taurus man may be slow but he always gets to the finish. When it comes to endurance, he takes first prize and he's unlikely to let her down. He'll find the Aries woman's passionate nature and sexual excitement stimulating but he won't expect to come to an exhausted, sweaty halt after just five minutes. He might not have the same level of energy as the Aries woman but he has bags more stamina. But they do have something in common: they are both very sexy creatures, so with her energy and his staying power, sex could be the main attraction of their relationship. However, he's a sensitive soul and doesn't take well to being strung along. He's also a stayer, so if she's unsure at the start, it would be better to stop sooner rather than later.

TAURUS MAN WITH **TAURUS WOMAN**

See pages 56–57.

TAURUS MAN WITH **GEMINI WOMAN**

In love: This relationship starts off rather touch-and-go, so the Gemini woman will feel as though she is in an earthquake—she'll know there's something going on, but won't be quite sure what it is until it has hit. As she finds it so hard to maintain one position for any length of time, there's something about Taurus man's steadfast, immovable charm that fascinates her. It's hard for her to believe that a human being can be so solid. From where she's standing, he looks like a statue of Adonis! She'll be drawn to him initially because he emanates a powerful masculinity that she could really get into, while he finds the witty, quick-thinking Gemini woman delightful enough to warrant further attention—although he may have trouble following her strange conversation down the twisting turns it sometimes takes. The Taurus man is intrigued by her excitability but can, at times, get a bit heavy in his demand for a simple, no-nonsense approach to life. Then she'll wonder where all the fun went and her light, flirty, and fickle manner can leave him feeling confused about where he stands in her heart. If she slows down and he speeds up so that they meet halfway, then he'll teach her the real meaning of romance and make her feel like a true woman, and she can give him a new perspective on fun and spontaneity.

In bed: The Taurus guy is all about manly strength and direct, no-fuss sexual contact, which won't leave much room for innuendo and intrigue, which are all part of the playful Gemini woman's seductive tool kit. She will always be fascinated by his firm, solid stance, and will never tire of playing with him, it's just that her rules and his don't match up, which could result in two grown people sulking because the other doesn't want to play the game properly! On occasion, and with some persistence, she could build his anticipation up to the point where he's raging with desire. However, the teasing temptress routine—trying to steer him first in this direction and then in that instead of spending a little longer in one place—could simply put him in a rage. He doesn't really like anyone toying with something as serious as his sensual pleasure, and he demands a solid and tangible response to his sexual advances. If he feels there's any doubt she's interested in pursuing an evening of passion, then the Taurus man will probably assume that she's not and will storm off, confused and hurt. The Gemini woman, on the other hand, loves the thrill of not quite knowing what's going to happen—too much certainty takes all the fun out of the moment when two people finally end up wrapped around each other.

TAURUS MAN WITH **CANCER WOMAN**

 In love: The Taurus man is rock-solid when it comes to love and the Cancer woman is sensitive, caring, and deeply impressed by his strength and calm. She'll know instantly that this is a man she could spend her life with. He'll be her anchor when the seas of emotion and insecurity get a bit rough and, like her Atlas, will keep her supported. Added to that, he's honest and won't play around with her, which fulfills perfectly her need for safety and security. The Cancer woman's ability to cater intuitively to his every need is very attractive to the Taurus man, who wants his woman to be a truly feminine provider of comfort, food, and affection. He wants to spend time cuddled up on a sofa with her, with tasty food and fine wine on the coffee table in front of them. This scene looks extremely seductive to the Cancer woman, because the safer and more secure she feels, the more she gives of her sweet and gentle heart. As he is so good at providing the luxurious, expensive, and romantic indulgences that make her feel special and loved, this is a mutually heart-warming relationship. Both are highly sentimental creatures, so anniversaries are unlikely to be forgotten. In fact, close friends and family will try to stay away because the cute intimacy and private exchanges between these two can get embarrassing for others. But this closeness is, indeed, the glue that binds them together.

 In bed: The Taurus man unleashed is not a force to underestimate. There's nothing delicate about the way he expresses his sexual urges. He'll grunt and groan like a bull but, aside from that, the Taurus man is an excellent lover. Lady Cancer will be a little bemused at first, but this uninhibited behavior is just what she's always dreamed of in a man. His unrestrained sexual manner allows her to abandon everything—fears, clothes, and anything else that could possibly stand in the way of total intimacy. The Taurus man will wrap his lunar lady up in his powerful embrace and press his body firmly against hers. Yes, he's very, very physical. She'll melt into his arms and feel so wanted and needed that she will be able to throw off any and all insecurities. She could even surprise herself with her new-found wanton sexiness. Nothing will stop her now. The Taurus man will have found his match and will be reveling in what he perceives as a stroke of luck. On occasion, he'll be clumsy and even a bit crude in his pillow talk. This would normally be a turn-off to the sensitive Cancer girl, but his gentle touch is comforting and he's so practiced at giving pleasure, that she may even find it funny. At any rate, a little giggling will only heighten her arousal—and his—but no teasing, please, he's in earnest.

TAURUS MAN WiTH **LEO WOMAN**

In love: The Taurus man can be extremely stubborn, but he'll find it very difficult to remain invulnerable to the charm and grace of a Leo woman. And she is very susceptible to a man with a discerning eye. A little flattery and an expensive gift will work wonders to win the heart of a Lioness, and the Taurus man will not be able to resist a woman who so graciously and gratefully receives his gifts and delights in his charms. He could, however, do without the demands and drama that the Lady Lion, who is a queen after all, feels are part of her remit. He won't rise to them, or bow and scrape, either. He sometimes finds the glitz-and-glamor thing to be too much flash and sparkle. He's a down-to-earth sort of guy and he's not used to the fast paced high life that Leo loves, whereas she's a sucker for pomp and pageantry and will fall for it, whoever provides it. The way he sees it, if he's going to offer her affection and attention, then there is absolutely no need for her to attract them from anyone else, for any reason! He just needs to learn that Leo is very loyal and doesn't like being mistrusted. He'll find it hard to resist her but she'll gain more from this relationship than she thinks, so it would be best for her not to take advantage of his good nature.

In bed: The Taurus man in bed is more sensual creature than wild beast. He likes to take his lovemaking long and slow, coming to a very, very gradual climax. The Leo lady will probably be in the multiples by then, but he'll keep going. She's not going to complain. After all, she loves his foreplay and the way he brings her to a frenzied climax. If she indulges him it won't stop there, but Lady Leo has all the patience of . . . well, a lioness. Once she has her prey in sight she'll chase him down and tear off his clothes with her teeth, then make a real meal of him. He won't know what's hit him! And again, when faced with such ardent passion, it's unlikely he's going to complain. So where's the problem? Well, they're both stubborn and they both like having things their own way; while he wants to slow her down and savor every sexy moment, she wants to gorge herself on passion. He'll find it hard to deal with her continued need for spontaneity, just as she'll resent any pressure on her to tone down her more flamboyant bedroom antics. However, the Leo lady doesn't mind the challenge. If she really has her heart set on the Bull, then she'll just keep going, which will naturally hot up his senses. Once he's turned on, it's near-impossible to turn him off, so even with all her drama, why would he want to try?

TAURUS mAN WiTH **ViRGO WOmAN**

In love: It may take a while for the Taurus man to get under the skin of the reticent Virgo woman, but when he does, it's in such a pleasant way. Neither of these two Earth signs are quick to fall in love, but once they do, they tend to remain true. He's persistent and if he has his heart set on her, he'll pursue her until she submits. However, her very feminine qualities should not be mistaken for signs of weakness. On the contrary, she is a rather discerning character and would not be persuaded to do anything unless she feels deep down that she wants to. If he gives her time, he'll earn her trust gradually, with his charm and utter determination. He'll know he has won her over, not just from the words she speaks, but from the feeling that she's truly given him her heart. His caring and purposeful nature will go a long way to helping her forget about his less attractive side—his stubbornness and pedantry, for example—just as her efficiency, good taste, and subtlety will allay any fears he has about her being highly strung and fussy. And while he doesn't take well to her need to analyze every tiny aspect of his character, he senses her hidden depths and passions and so is happy to indulge her occasionally. The Virgo woman is seduced by this man, who is so full of romantic gestures and sensual affection, and she values his calm, powerful presence, especially when she's feeling nervous and unsure of herself.

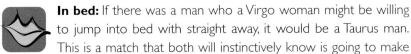 **In bed:** If there was a man who a Virgo woman might be willing to jump into bed with straight away, it would be a Taurus man. This is a match that both will instinctively know is going to make fireworks in their otherwise down-to-earth lives. It's one that will certainly ruffle a few sheets! Since a Taurus man is so very determined in the pursuit of his hedonistic pleasures, it's no surprise that sex comes top of his list, particularly sex with a Virgo woman. He'll work very hard to learn where her erogenous zones are and will know instinctively just what to do with them once he's found them. What is more, he won't mind if it takes her a while to get with the program. He enjoys his studies very much. It's these

important little details that the Virgo woman really appreciates. She might act the hard task master, insisting that practice makes perfect, but, with her immediate response to every correctly placed touch, she also makes his job easy. It's true that the male Bull is rough, ready, and a little crude when he's feeling horny—which Bulls generally are—while the demure and modest Virgo lady is apparently more refined, but it should be remembered that she is as earthy as he is and just as capable of mucking in when there is deliciously dirty work to be done (though she'll be the first to head for the shower). This is marathon lovemaking at its very best!

TAURUS MAN WITH LIBRA WOMAN

 In love: It is in the Taurus man that the Libra woman finds a partner who will appreciate her talents and refined behavior. The Libra woman has an innate appreciation for all fine things and her attractive appearance says it all. The Taurus man will easily develop a love of and appreciation for everything that she stands for. He'll be romantic, never forgetting her birthday or anniversary, and candlelit dinners for two will be a regular feature of their relationship. He is, of course, entranced by her effortless femininity and by the way she always asks him for his opinion and considers his feelings before making a decision. She, in her turn, will be intrigued by his ability to relate to her feminine qualities: he will go shopping with her and offer opinions on female issues without finding these things threatening to his masculinity—which underlines that masculinity even more. He adores being made to feel as if he's the epitome of strength and manliness, just as she loves the feeling of peace and safety he gives her. It's a relationship that has all the elements of togetherness that they both yearn for. Both signs are ruled by the planet Venus, so love, beauty, and art are powerful motivating forces in their lives. Their shared abode would be a sumptuous symphony of good taste and comfort: the eye would delight in its harmonious play of color, texture, and light. Taureans can be stubborn though, so there may be times when the Libra woman will have to rely heavily on her skills of diplomacy.

 In bed: Bed is where this couple differs, and the differences could either be looked upon as enjoyable, enlightening, and erotic, or as something that finally rubs both of them up the wrong way— literally. Making love means very different things to each of them, but both are pretty willing to please, so making adjustments to suit the other will certainly keep a smile on their faces for some time afterward! Friends and family will wonder what's going on! The Taurus man is sensual and earthy, with a powerful need for physical contact. She is airy, and enjoys indulging in the fantasy realm of romantic ideals. What turns her on is not only the gentle touch of his hands on her body, but the meeting of minds and quest for poetic love expressed through whispered words. However, her desire for a mental union may leave him a little bewildered, just as his purely physical approach may have her shying away. "Surely he loves me for my mind?" cries the Libra lady. "Can't she see how much I love her by the way I'm longing to get her into bed?'' bemoans the Taurus man. This is where the whole loved-up Venusian relationship can fall apart, but since they're both creative, it's unlikely to do so. Feeding strawberries dipped in chocolate to one another while lying in bed will help spur on the process of getting it on, and the heat will rapidly rise from this point onward!

TAURUS MAN WITH SCORPIO WOMAN

In love: Being opposites in the zodiac, the Scorpio woman and her Taurus man are like the Yin-Yang symbol, each half containing a minute essence of the other while also perfectly reflecting the whole. They seem familiar, even directly after meeting, because it's something they recognize in one another. It's a partnership that just feels right, like a hand in a well-fitting glove. They cling together in the sure knowledge that they complement and complete one another. With a Taurus man by her side, the Scorpio woman can feel the safety and security that are so important to her, while he can revel in the deep well of emotional devotion that she will keep in reserve only for him. From the moment they meet, they feel a mutual desire to indulge themselves in the finer things in life—there is a hedonistic quality to the relationship that makes no apology for the passionate pursuit of love, affection, and rich pleasure. However, the Taurus man is very possessive, while the Scorpio lady can become viciously jealous. As long as they stick to one another, these qualities can work perfectly together, but if one of them comes unstuck, there will be an almighty battle of wills. And as they are both incredibly stubborn, there could be harsh words followed by long spells of silence. But with understanding and mutual respect, this partnership will stand on very firm foundations and has the promise of getting better and better.

In bed: When it comes to the sensual appetite department, the Taurus man and Scorpio woman have met their match. A log fire, a bottle of champagne, a box of rich liqueur chocolates, and music playing gently in the background… They'll probably fall asleep some time before dawn, only to wake when the sun has risen, and gently but intensely make love all over again. It's not everyone who can fulfill the sexually savvy Scorpio woman's appetite for erotic pleasure, but she loves it when her man gets down and dirty, and this one seems to have it all going for him! He is one hundred percent male and as solid and steady as a rock. His animalistic moves bring out the beast in her, yet he can also be controlled and measured and he has the stamina to stay with her as she cries out with delight—it's her way of showing true intimacy. For him, her mysterious femininity and liquid touch have an ecstatic quality that quenches his thirst for physical union and will have him drowning in the depths of her loving body. He wants to taste and savor every bit of her, while she could devour him whole. They are both such hungry lovers, it's difficult to tell who will eat up whom. But one thing is certain: they will never get bored with one another. For better or for worse, every entanglement will have a sexual overtone.

TAURUS MAN WITH **SAGITTARIUS WOMAN**

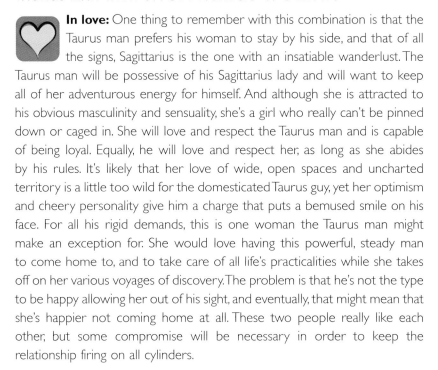

In love: One thing to remember with this combination is that the Taurus man prefers his woman to stay by his side, and that of all the signs, Sagittarius is the one with an insatiable wanderlust. The Taurus man will be possessive of his Sagittarius lady and will want to keep all of her adventurous energy for himself. And although she is attracted to his obvious masculinity and sensuality, she's a girl who really can't be pinned down or caged in. She will love and respect the Taurus man and is capable of being loyal. Equally, he will love and respect her, as long as she abides by his rules. It's likely that her love of wide, open spaces and uncharted territory is a little too wild for the domesticated Taurus guy, yet her optimism and cheery personality give him a charge that puts a bemused smile on his face. For all his rigid demands, this is one woman the Taurus man might make an exception for. She would love having this powerful, steady man to come home to, and to take care of all life's practicalities while she takes off on her various voyages of discovery. The problem is that he's not the type to be happy allowing her out of his sight, and eventually, that might mean that she's happier not coming home at all. These two people really like each other, but some compromise will be necessary in order to keep the relationship firing on all cylinders.

In bed: Both the Taurus man and the Sagittarius woman love sex! And the initial attraction between them is very strong because they sense in each other someone who is as unabashed and frank about their sexual desires as they are. When they get it together, sex could be raunchy, definitely very physical, and oddly satisfying. He will love the way she navigates herself around his body with her hungry curiosity, and she can't help but lose herself in his intense masculine strength. They will both respond with an equal amount of ardor and fervent passion, and indeed, if they're willing to work at it, they could build up an intense little inferno in the bedroom. There could be just one problem: while the tenacious Taurus man isn't at all work-shy and is happy to persist in the pursuit of pleasure, the Lady Archer needs more immediate results. Her attention is capable of waning, while he can stay focussed for long periods of time. She can be ready for it anytime, anywhere, and she enjoys the spontaneous adventure. He, however, wants it in a big, comfortable bed, at around bedtime, which means that, in the long run, sex could get a little too predictable for her taste. Compromise and negotiation are key factors in keeping this love alive. If she can have her way for half the week and he for the other half, this sexual union could provide a very colorful array of scrumptious erotic choice.

TAURUS MAN WITH **CAPRICORN WOMAN**

In love: Love between a Capricorn woman and a Taurus man comes easy. It just feels so natural to be in one another's company. He has all the qualities that she admires and wants in a partner—a strong character, good taste, creativity, and downright desirability—just as she, with her cool head, practicality, and inspiring character, appeals to him. His sixth sense lets him know that hidden under her controlled exterior is an intensely passionate soul just waiting to be released by the romantic security he can provide. It would be easy for these two Earth signs to start their relationship by first striking up a friendship, and it would be obvious to both that there was something more intimate going on beneath the surface. But both prefer to take their time in getting to know their potential partners, finding out what makes them happy or sad, mad or glad. They don't trust flash-in-the-pan flirtations; they want to be sure that the infatuation is more than just a passing phase. Neither is willing to make a premature commitment but once they do decide to hand over their hearts, it will be for certain. So while they shouldn't expect fireworks from day one, they should feel the strange, low rumbling that warns them that the earth is about to move. This just feels so right that they'll never be in any doubt that it's a match made in heaven. His love makes her feel deeply secure.

In bed: If the Capricorn woman ever wants to feel like a sex object—which actually happens all the time, though she'd never let on!—then the Taurus man can oblige. She'll be his sex object, but one that is loved, adored, and respected all at the same time. Each of these highly physical people can find in the other someone who yearns for the sort of touch that cuts to the chase and doesn't waste hours on verbal foreplay that is clearly only a prelude to something else. They've already spent the time getting to know each other during the courting stage, and they will undoubtedly be constantly aware of the nearly tangible sexual tension that exists between them, so once they've made the decision to go for it, they go for it! In fact, it's possible for these two to do all their communicating without using any words. They have an unspoken agreement to abandon themselves to physical pleasure. It's as though each trusts the other to do all that's required to reach a climactic union. This relationship is so sexy that it will be amazing if they find time for anything else. If you could be a fly on the wall, it would be an incredible turn-on to see how their bodies are drawn together like powerful magnets, and cannot be separated until they have both reached a climax of incredible pleasure.

TAURUS mAN WiTH **AQUARiUS WOmAN**

 In love: Both the Aquarius woman and the Taurus man are rather stubborn and opinionated, so sometimes it can be fun for them to find someone to flex their muscles against. The Taurus man generally knows what he's talking about because it takes him some time to form an opinion and this appeals to the Aquarius woman because she likes a lover who she can learn from. However, as she also likes to think around corners, it will be difficult for her to get him to go along with some of her more zany ideas. He is very conservative, whereas she is original and totally idiosyncratic. She will want to smash through convention, while he feels safe playing by the rules. It is possible that these two could fall in love with each other, but it might feel as if they've done it against their better judgment. Love is not free and easy for an Aquarius woman with a Taurus man; it's more like hard work. But then again, once they've tasted the pleasures that each has to offer, coming apart may prove to be even harder work! The Aquarius lady could intellectualize for hours on end about whether to stay together or not, and certainly the Taurus man could listen. In the end, they might decide that it's simply easier to stay together and enjoy the love they have! But whatever they decide, whether together or apart, this is a relationship with impact. They won't ever forget one another.

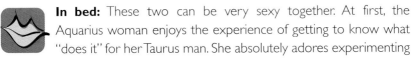 **In bed:** These two can be very sexy together. At first, the Aquarius woman enjoys the experience of getting to know what "does it" for her Taurus man. She absolutely adores experimenting and trying out new things, and she'll want to please this man because he's so deliciously happy when he's making love. He is so fascinated by her electric response to his touch that he just wants to touch her over and over again. However, what she responds to one minute doesn't necessarily do it

for her the next. Variety is a spice of her life, but it can be variety within just one relationship, so long as that relationship is flexible enough. But in the long run, the Lady Water-Bearer could be too physically aloof for her Bull lover, and too unpredictable. One day she is compellingly committed to engaging in erotic pleasure and the next, faced with her Taurus lover panting and reaching out to her from the bed, she'll assume that he's injured himself and simply wants help getting up. This kind of behavior has a very destabilizing effect on the sensitive male ego of the physically demanding Taurus man; he just can't understand how she can be so inconstant in her desires. He knows that she's not frigid and how passionate she can be, yet sometimes she seems so cold. He needs lots of affection; she needs lots of variety. The sex may become so predictable that she ends up lying back thinking about the shopping list while he lies on top getting on with the job.

TAURUS mAN WiTH PiSCES WOmAN

In love: Here is a love that the Pisces woman can trust. It looks like the one she's been waiting for all her life. He's romantic, protective, and so much like a real prince. And the Pisces woman appears to have all that the Taurus man could want . . . he thinks that he has finally found someone he can control! He'll have to think again, but she won't let him know that she has a mind of her own; he'll have to figure it out for himself. Meanwhile, he has all the strength and sensitivity she requires in a man and he is so susceptible to her dreamy, romantic allure that it won't take her long to capture his heart completely. She'll enjoy being spoiled by a Taurus man who simply adores buying her flowers and chocolates, and taking her away for romantic weekends. But that first flush of romance is not going to last forever, for then up steps Mr. Practicality—the man who wants to save his money by keeping her barefoot and pregnant in the kitchen, and making the meals for which he has set the table so beautifully. If she longs for security, then she'll happily submit because she knows that there will still be occasions when he'll whisk her off to a wonderful restaurant where she can dress up and relive her dream. But some Pisces ladies will feel that the bubble has burst and will be totally disillusioned with the loss of their romantic ideals. If the Pisces woman does decide to give her heart to him, he'll treasure it beyond measure.

In bed: When this relationship becomes sexual—and it won't take long—that's when it really becomes a relationship. She can have him on his knees with just a glance—a very convenient position as far as she's concerned—and he might even make a proposal (indecent or otherwise!) while he's down there. These two should get a big, firm mattress and heaps of feather cushions, because they'll be spending a lot of time in the bedroom. This is where they can achieve an intimacy that's both comforting and fulfilling. They will adore being enveloped in their private world and wrapped around each other's bodies. It's the physical closeness that is so important to the Taurus man, and the emotional connection that anchors the Pisces woman's heart. Any time that other aspects of the relationship are breaking down, blissful togetherness between the sheets will halt the damage and make their love blossom all over again. She is more than willing to give herself up and be totally immersed in his strongly sensual needs. She has such an erotic imagination that he might fear losing himself in her soft naked body, yet it also gives him a sense of the strength of his masculinity. Her total surrender makes him an even more ardent and skillful lover—and that suits her just fine!